GOOGLE CHROMEBOOK MANUAL

A Simplified Guide on How to use
Chromebook from soups to Nuts

Benjamin F. Trigger

GOOGLE CHROMEBOOK MANUAL

A Simplified Guide on How to use Chromebook from Soups to Nuts

Benjamin F. Trigger

This book is dedicated to all Chromebook users/owners

Contents

Introduction

You probably recently got a Chromebook. Big congratulations. Undoubtedly, Google's ChromeBook has been around for so long now, but it has mostly taken a backseat to the company's stable of Android devices. With the latest release of ChromeBooks, Google has finally given this new computing platform the attention it deserves, and it will grow by leaps and bounds in the years to come. The ChromeBook is a not only a new series of devices, but a new computing paradigm.

The ChromeBook can do almost anything that more expensive PCs are capable of. It's everything you need, and none of what you don't.

. This book provides you with all you really need to optimize ChromeBook; from setup to tricks, troubleshooting and shortcuts.

What is a

Chromebook?

Everyone knows the traditional PC and Mac but

he Chromebook is that laptop that's still oblivious to many. But in recent years this device has gained popularity and it's one you have to try out. It's no different than a laptop in form.

In fact, it's just a laptop. But the only thing is that most of the versions of the device come in smaller sizes. But the keyboard, the screen, the touchpad make it qualify as a laptop. The shock comes when you power on the Chromebook and you then see something different than what you are used to. The look and design of a laptop's display are attributed to the operating system.

It's why Mac computers running on the macOS will always be different from PCs running on Windows operating system. So you should expect that the Chromebook will be different because it runs on the Chrome OS.

So to give a straight definition, I'll say that the Chromebook is a laptop device that functions on Google's Chrome OS. But the question now is that what is the Chrome OS? The Chrome OS is an extension of the Chrome browser but functions on the Chromebook.

Chrome is very popular and I don't think that one wouldn't know what it is. But for those at the backseat; Chrome is a browser created by Google. It works on computers and smartphones and it has risen to become one of the most widely used browsers

If you have turned on your Chromebook, you would have noticed that the Chrome OS is not just a browser like Chrome. And you are right, the Chrome OS is more than Chrome. It's an operating system and it works like one. Together with Chromebook, you'll be able to install games and apps on the device.

To say the truth, the Chromebook is an awesome device but here's the thing. The OS is not like the one that many apps and sites know. Many apps recognize the PC and Mac but the Chromebook is somewhat strange. As a result, you might not be able to use some apps and programs.

But one thing you can do about this is find out if there's the web browser equivalent of the app so that you can just access it on the browser. If you have mobile app version available, there's still hope. Now's when you roll your eyes and start to wonder how a mobile app will work on the PC.

The thing is that when the Chrome OS was created it was made to function well with the Google Play Store. And you would agree that the Play Store has a lot of apps. So if an app is in the Play Store, it stands chance of being able to work on the Chromebook. This is for some Chromebooks, not all can do this.

Unlike most laptops, the Chromebook doesn't cost that much. If you have a tight budget, you should be able to squeeze some change to buy the device if you have an interest.

Chromebook Set up Process

If you just try to use the power button to turn on the Chromebook the first time when you got it, it didn't take long before you realized that was not the way to go. You should at least first connect it to the charger and when it starts getting power, you can turn it on.

This is the step to follow if you got your Chromebook spanking new. But if it's used or like refurbished you wouldn't need to go through this process

Step 1

Sign in to Google

When you Chromebook boots, you will need to sign in to Google first. Singing in is not hard and it's just the same as signing in to Gmail or the normal Chrome browser. When you sign in, your themes, bookmarks and others will be synced.

Step 2
Download apps

The newer Chromebooks give you the opportunity to access the Google Play Store. And while i would love to say that all apps on the Play Store can work on the Chromebook that is not the case. But most of the apps will work. Like Lightroom, Word and others.

Then there are also other apps that you can use to take your Chrome experience to another level. You can try Netflix, Comixology or Amazon Video.

Step 3
Include a second account to the device

If you have a friend that tends to use your computers regularly and you know that now that you have the brand new Chromebook, they'll be dying to try it out, you use the option to add a second account. They should be able to use this as long the account is a Google account. If it's not, then they may need to create a Google account and add it to your Chromebook

Step 4

Feel the touchpad

Yes, you can just connect a mouse to the Chromebook and use that to navigate but why not try out the touchpad instead. It's there and it's easy to use. If you use a Windows laptop previously, then getting a hang of the Chromebook's touchpad may be a bit tricky at first but in a while, you'll get used to it and soon become a big fan.

Step 5

Secure your Chromebook with a lock

If you have a tight security password, you should use it to secure your laptop. It the best way you can secure your data. While it won't be the most convenient method to use to sign in, it's the best thing you can do to secure your Chromebook.

Chromebook Tips and Tricks

One of the top features of the Chromebook is that the device is simple. And it's true, it really is simple. It's not like the other big computers that have got a ton of complex stuff. But that does not mean that there are no advanced options for those who want to do more than the normal.

Doing the normal can get boring and you're just left feeling like there's more to the Chromebook than meets the eye and you're right, there is. These tips and tricks will enable make the best of the Chromebook.

Ranging from getting the hang of the mysterious Chromebook Launcher to utilizing the shelf at the lower area of the screen to making use of the web to the fullest, you'll become a power user by the time you're done with this section.

The launcher

The launcher on the Chrome OS is the interface that you can call a drawer. It comes up when you hit the Search key. You can also use the circle symbol at the left corner of the screen. It's a great tool that you can use to search for stuff on your computer.

When it shows up, you can just start to type in queries. With this, you can find apps quickly, launch websites or get answers to some questions from it.

It's also a converter

The launcher isn't only used to bring up apps or find files on the system. You can also use it to do some calculations and conversions. If you would like to test out its powers, you can start by typing in your questions.

You can do basic conversions like 18 feet to meters or 34 inches to centimeters. You can also try out its calculation features, 158 x 45 or 1240/8 and put the system to work

Page last opened

This next tip is going to be useful if you use the same Google account for both your phone and computer. If you open up a page or article recently on your phone, you just have to look at the top area of the launcher on the Chromebook.

You should see the heading of the page show up as a suggested title just under the search bar for the Chromebook's launcher. It's a great way to continue where you left off on your smartphone device. Just click it and continue reading

Send the shelf into hiding

You should be familiar with the shelf by now. This is the row that shows the items you've pinned and you can find it at the bottom of the screen. There's a trick you can use to hide the shelf.

Right click the row or press and hold depending on the way you use the Chromebook. Then choose the option for **Auto Hide Shelf.** Now the shelf will always disappear when there's an open app or window. But if you hover on it or swipe from the lower part of the screen, it will appear again.

But whether you have an app open or not, this shelf will always be visible if you are viewing the desktop.

Access the launcher like Android

If you use the tablet mode for the Chromebook most of the time, here's another way to bring up the launcher easily. Though you can access it from an open screen this feature is a hidden gesture that not many users know about.

You just need to swipe upwards from the bottom of the screen in an empty area. I don't know if you noticed but it's just the way you do it with Android for Pixel smartphones. When you do this for the Chromebook, the launcher will show up.

Launch an app in a snap

Here's another cool one you've never heard of. You can launch an app on the shelf by using the Alt key. It's not every time you'll be in the mood to slide around with your touchpad and select an item from the shelf manually. You set it to be in the shelf because it's your favorites but if you can't access it easily, it kind of defeats the purpose.

But when you use the Alt key together with the number that matches the item's position on the shelf, you'll fire it up quickly. So if an item is no 5 on the launcher, the shortcut will be **Alt + 5** and if it the third app, it'll be **Alt + 3**, and it goes on for the rest of the items

More shortcuts

You can find out other program-related shortcuts you can use for specific apps. If you use the Chromebook in laptop mode, you just have to right-click an app whether in the main launcher or the shelf and the options will be shown.

If that app is an Android app, there'll be more options for shortcuts relating to that app.

Bring up the quick setting quickly

As of now, the Chrome OS is equipped with a Quick Settings menu that looks like an android phone. It's not just the Quick Settings, the Notification panel to at the bottom right area of the screen is also Android-like.

If you would like to access this area without sliding with the mouse, you can just hit **Shift + Alt + N** and it'll come up.

One click, one sweep

Another resemblance to the android is the ability to clear away notifications with just one click. If you have a lot of notifications on the computer it can be very annoying when they crowd out the panel. There's a way to clear them fast but it's not the easiest thing to find.

1. Open up the **Notifications** panel
2. Move to the very bottom of the list
3. When you get to the last notification, find the **Clear All** button and select it.

So instead of attending to them one after the other, this just clears them all quickly

Scribble away

Do you have your Chromebook device with a stylus? If you do, then you'll be happy to know that you can take notes right from the lock screen when you have the **Google Keep** app. Sometimes, you just want to scribble down something without having to open the device in a grand style

If you install the app, you just have to enter the device settings, select the section for **Stylus** and make sure that you have the **Lock Screen Note-Taking** option enabled. When it's enabled, there'll be an icon on the lock screen that lets you know that you can start taking notes.

Open new tabs quick

If you wanted to open a new tab, you will have to right click then choose the option for open in new tab. It's a great method and it's better than copying the link then pasting in a window manually.

But there's a much faster and better way to go about it. If you would like to open a link in a new tab on your Chromebook, you just click the link with 3 fingers with the touchpad and it will be opened in that new tab.

Close tabs in a whim

Yes you can just use the **X** button at top to close any tab but it's always cool to have these shortcuts. This one will also require you to use 3 fingers. If you would like to close a tab on the Chromebook quickly, navigate to the title bar and click the touchpad with 3 fingers

Open windows quick

It's very normal to surf the web with your Chromebook and before you realize it the whole window becomes full with open tabs. If you'd like to open more tabs can just go ahead and open them in that same window but that will just get things squeezed and running slow.

I like to keep a maximum of about 6 – 7 tab open per window. So when it's getting past that, I either delete useless tabs or if all are important, I just open new ones in a new window. If you'd like to do this without wasting much time, you can just hit **Ctrl + N** and you have yourself a new window

Add to shelf

Here's a great way to add a site to the shelf for easy access

1. Enter the Chrome menu as the site is opened up
2. Select **More Tools**
3. Select the **Create Shortcut Option**

Reduce the keyboard size

When you set the keyboard to tablet mode you get a very large keyboard. While some may be okay with this and may even love it, it can be too much to handle for others. If you belong to the second group, you can reduce the size of said keyboard.

Select the second icon at the keyboard's top row. (box in a box icon). This will reduce the keyboard's size to one that it is within thumb reach. You can also move around the screen

Write with stylus

Select the first icon at the top row of the keyboard. It takes the shape of a squiggle. If you choose the icon, a canvas will be opened to you. You can then write with your stylus. You can also try to write with your hand but it'll better to stick with your stylus

More from the stylus

This is another one for the stylus users. If you have a Chromebook that's with a stylus, you can select the stylus menu that's at the lower right corner of the screen. It's just at the notifications panel area. When you select this option, you can be able to even use the stylus to its fullest.

Use the task manager

It's very common for the laptop to run slowly. This can be if there are many apps running at the same time. To remedy the slow effect, you can slide into the task manager and end some processes. This task manager process can also prove to be useful if there's an app that's misbehaving. During such times, even the Close button for that app can become unavailable.

You can summon the task manager quickly when you use the combination of the **Search key + Esc key**. Select this and the task manager will be opened.

Keyboard lights

If you have your Chromebook with the modern type of keyboard, that is the keyboard with backlights, there's a quick shortcut to reduce the light intensity. Though it's always great have a shining light at the back of the keyboard especially during the dark hours of the night, it can take a toll on the battery and it will run down quickly.

If you would like to reduce it or increase, hit **Alt + Brightness keys**. Use the **Up** key to increase the light and the **Down** to reduce the light

Log in to Chromebook-banned sites.

Want to hear a funny story? There are websites that still think the Chromebook is not a standard computer. Which is totally unbelievable because, the Chromebook is well and working. But if that's how they those organizations wish to do their thing, there's nothing we can do about it.

Or is there? You see, if they can't allow us to enter because of our Chrome OS, don't you think we would be granted access if we made them think that we were using another operating system and not the Chrome OS? I think so too and that's why we have the **User Agent Switcher**. This is an extension you can install on the Chromebook. With it, you can disguise your operating system and trick the sites into thinking that you are a genuine Windows user or another OS.

Dictation for the Chromebook

Who is in the mood for some voice-to-text? I know I am and you should be too. It's a great way to optimize your Chromebook for dictation. There's the microphone icon on keyboard that shows up on the screen. You can find this when you set the keyboard to tablet mode.

It's very easy to start using the on-screen keyboard dictation feature but you can also set up the physical keyboard,

1. Go to the **Settings**
2. Scroll down to the bottom and select **Advanced**
3. Scroll and select the option for **Manage Accessibility** just beneath **Accessibility**.
4. Turn on the **Enable Dictation** option
5. With this, the microphone icon should be shown at the bottom of the screen.

Text Blaze

Another extension you can install on your Chromebook is the **Text Blaze.** It's a cool extension that can make your device smarter. This will enable you to create custom shortcuts for the words and phrases you type out commonly.

You can also set that an email address will be typed out automatically when you enter in a particular shortcut. It's a good idea to experiment with the template and see how much time it saves you.

Caps Lock manipulation

If you are new to the Chromebook, you would have certainly been shocked when you found out there wasn't a Caps Lock key on the laptop. And of course you miss the key now. If you would still like to make use of the key, just use the **Alt + Search key** combo to give you the same result

You just press this and you have your texts in uppercase. If you would like to stop the uppercasing and return to normal mode, hit the same **Alt + Search**. If that doesn't satisfy you, there's a much permanent way

Return the Caps Lock to its rightful place

If you really want to the Caps Lock key back on your device, you can also set it to be on the keyboard permanently. For some, the **Alt + Search** key method is just enough and they can manage with it. But for others like me, we'll like something more stable.

But this will have you sacrificing the Search key. You will need to choose; Caps Lock or Search key. This is because we'll be swapping the keys so that the Search performs the function of the Caps

1. Enter the **Settings**
2. Choose **Keyboard** when you get to the **Device** segment

Apply Smart Lock

With the Smart Lock option, you can use your Android phone to unlock your Chromebook. Google just has a way of connecting its products and services together. If you would like to try this out, you can just enable Smart Lock by

1. Going to **Settings**
2. Select the **Connected Devices** area.

With this, you just need to have your Android phone nearby and you'll be able to use to unlock your laptop.

Enable guest browsing

We all have that friend that always fancies using your computer to surf the web. Sometimes, we don't mind letting them use it but on other times, you may have an opened tab you would rather not let them see. The Guest Mode is there to help.

They can access this at the top of the browser's title bar and when it's enabled, the browser will be sent into something like an incognito mode. Also, history won't be stored and accounts won't be left signed in. Which is totally cool because when they are gone it would be like they were never there.

Restrict sign in

On your Chromebook, you may not like the idea of people just using your device. The Chromebook allows this by default but you can restrict it.

1. Go to the **Settings**
2. Look for the **Manage Other People** section
3. Find the option that reads **Restrict Sign In To The Following Users**
4. Now you just have to set your people and give permission to just them

Take it back to the lock screen

Don't tell me you just leave your Chromebook on the same document screen and walk away to attend to other matters. Yes, you don't want to shut off the device completely but at least take it to the lock screen so that wondering eyes don't find out what you've been working on.

If you think it would take forever to bring up the lock screen, just press the **Search key + L**.

Sign out fast

That's one way to close off your work screen but if you would like to completely sign out, you can use the **Ctrl + Shift + Q** shortcut. Before you press this shortcut, you want to make sure you save any of your progress because it will close all the windows open. But it's still a good way to shut everything down and it works no matter the nook or cranny you are in the Chromebook.

Do not disturb

Apps just have a way of annoying you with silly notifications. You hear a beep just to find out that it's something trivial. If you would you would love to have to peace and quiet in your life,

1. Fire up the **Notifications** panel
2. Select the **Do Not Disturb** icon. The circular icon with a dash in the center

Another browser

If the Chrome makes you sick, you aren't stuck on it. Though it is unlikely Chrome will have such an effect on you as the browser is just simply just amazing but there are exceptions to the rule

Android apps can work on Chromebook so you can slide into the Play Store, find your favorite web browser and install. You have a lot to choose from but these are ones you can try; Firefox, Dolphin, Opera, Puffin.

Display on a big screen

Chromebooks now have the opportunity of being displayed on a much larger screen. Something like the Chromecast TV screen. You may make use of this in your office, hotel room conference center.

If you would like to mirror the display of your computer on the TV screen, you just

1. Go to the **Quick Setting** panel
2. Select the **Cast** option
3. Casts in the Wi-Fi network will be pulled up and you can start mirroring

Access computers

If you would like to access another computer, you just have to try out the Chromebook Remote Desktop. It's a great way to access computer running of Mac, Windows, Linux or even the same Chrome OS. Plus you don't need to purchase some expensive software.

Taking a screenshot

If you would like to take a screenshot on the Chromebook, you should know that there are 3 ways to go about it so just pick one that best for what you would like to achieve.

To take a shot of the entire screen when using you Chromebook in tablet mode you can press the Power button + Volume down buttons. Use Ctrl + Overview key when the Chromebook is in laptop mode. To capture a specific area, use Ctrl + Shift + Overview key.

Night light

Are you still using your Chromebook late into the night? You know you should catch some sleep but you may have some deadline to meet. So at least turn on night light mode.

This will help reduce the strain that the normal light of the screen will put on your eyes. Enter the **Quick Setting** panel and select the **Night Light** button. If you would like to you can do some customizations to the setting.

Disclaimer

This book is not an overall guide to Chromebook tricks
and troubleshooting

About The Author

Benjamin Trigger been writing tech related books for some 15 years now. Some of his research materials have appeared in international magazines and blogs.

www.ingramcontent.com/pod-product-compliance
Lightning Source LLC
Chambersburg PA
CBHW031248050326
40690CB00007B/1008